OUT OF THE *Darkness*
AND INTO THE *Light*

OUT OF THE  Darkness
AND INTO THE Light

It's Never Too Late to Change

KAMMY HOWARD

authorHOUSE®

AuthorHouse™
1663 Liberty Drive
Bloomington, IN 47403
www.authorhouse.com
Phone: 1-800-839-8640

First published by AuthorHouse   09/20/2011

ISBN: 978-1-4634-3050-4 (sc)
ISBN: 978-1-4634-3049-8 (ebk)

Library of Congress Control Number: 2011913151

Printed in the United States of America

Any people depicted in stock imagery provided by Thinkstock are models, and such images are being used for illustrative purposes only.
Certain stock imagery © Thinkstock.

This book is printed on acid-free paper.

Because of the dynamic nature of the Internet, any web addresses or links contained in this book may have changed since publication and may no longer be valid. The views expressed in this work are solely those of the author and do not necessarily reflect the views of the publisher, and the publisher hereby disclaims any responsibility for them.

CONTENTS

Dedication to God

My first dedication is to the Lord my Savior Jesus Christ in heaven. I can't thank you enough for bringing me out of the darkness and in to the light. I know it was you who did it. Thank you for allowing me to write this book for you and to help other people. Thank you for all that you do for me and my family. Amen.

I love you

Dedication to my Mom

My second dedication is to my mom Debbie Perkins who has been my rock and my inspiration. She prayed for me for 14 years while I was in and out of my addiction. She used to tell me it's never too late to change and God gave her strength to do so when I need it the most. Thank you God for giving my mom that strength to do that when I know it was hard for her to see me that way. So never give up on yourself or any one that you love. In our society today, few woman have had the privilege to be mothered and even fewer woman have had a mother who they can love, respect and honor.

Words will never be able to express how much my mom has been there for me no matter what good, bad or indifferent. The woman and everything I am is because of her. Thank you God that I am the daughter of Debbie Lynn Perkins

I love you mom!

Dedication to my Kids

My third dedication to the most wonderful kids a mom could ever have. Timmy, Leah and I dedicate this book to show them that no matter what they go through never give up on your dreams see them through because I know you can do whatever it is that you set your mind too! Just like I did!

I love both of you guys!
Love Mom!

Special Thanks

First and for most to the Lord, thank you for seeing me through. Thanks to my husband for giving me encouragement. Thank you Bonnie Reinholtz for reading it and telling me what you as a reader would like to hear more of. Thank you Grandpa Jerry Nelson for telling me what needs to be talk about in the book Thank you Angela Nobao for taking the time to read it and telling me that it is not done there, something missing. Thank you Aunt Eva Jones for taking a glance at it and telling me it's good. Thanks to the people at AuthorHouse for helping me every step of the way. Thanks to all who read my book.

Introduction

This book is about my life and how I overcame the many hardships I have been through, I hope my experience will be of help to anyone who reads about it. This is a true story about when I was in turmoil and didn't know why. I kept making the same mistakes over and over. Nonetheless, each time I learned something new. It took me years, but eventually I figured out how to go about things differently. One thing I learned is to never have anger about something that happens. Anger just builds resentment and guilt. These reactions only hold you back from doing what you really want to do in life.

Chapter 1

My Childhood

When I was little, my mom was always working. At that time, my parents were divorced, so my mom had to be *both* parents. According to my mother, the reason they got divorced was because my dad was growing pot in the house. I guess I really never had a father growing up. My mom worked so hard to take care of me, I remember going to the babysitter all the time. Despite that, I always felt my mom's love, and to this day, I still do.

I am an only child, which had its ups and downs. Now I have stepbrothers, which is great, but from time to time growing up, I wondered what it was like to have a real sister or brother. The downside to it was I never had anybody to talk to—when times were good or bad. I always had to find ways to entertain myself. The upside to it was I always got what I wanted, so I don't know which was better—the ups *or* the downs!

I was always active as a child. In fact, I was *hyperactive* as a child and always in trouble at school, because I would jump on desks and do other things of that nature. I was put on Ritalin, a medication that counteracts hyperactivity disorders, but my mom thought it turned me into a zombie, so she took me off of that. We went back to the doctor, and he suggested we try something else—so I started to drink coffee at four years old! I don't know, maybe it worked, because as I got older, it got better. Now I'm just *active*. I also had a learning disability and was in special classes for slow learners, but this also went away as I grew up. I was always good with numbers, remembering music, and so forth, so I wasn't that slow!

When I was seventeen years old, I reunited with my father. He had started coming around to talk to my mom and me. I really didn't know what to say to him! I wanted to tell him so much and ask him so much, but I froze up. He would take us out to eat from time to time, and he would always take me to the skating rink when I wanted to go. For fourteen years of my life, he had not been there. Now, I was doing my own thing, and my mom was doing her own thing.

I remember he would make me write these sentences. I hated doing them—I am talking like five hundred of them every time I saw him! He would make me do that, and I never could understand why. Now I do—when I got reunited with my father, it happened at school. So I guess my father asked my school how was I doing in my classes, and they must have told him what needed improvement. That's why he made me write those sentences!

I had asked my mom how he found me, and she told me that since she was the sole caretaker when they got divorced, she had to garnishee his wages to take care of me. So that's how he found me, through the public records. I never could understand why my mom had to shop at garage sales; now I know why.

There are a lot of things that I couldn't understand, but sometimes it's good not to know about things that you don't understand when you are young. What you don't know won't hurt you. But what you do know might build resentment toward that person that you are asking about. So I am kind of glad that I found out about my dad later on in life, because I never could imagine having resentment toward my mom. My mom is my life, because she has been there for me *no matter what.*

Chapter 2

Getting To Know My Dad When I Really Wanted To

"Never go without saying 'I love you' to someone that you love." That's what my mom always told me, because you never know when it's their time to *really* go! Life is so short, so never take anything for granted. We are always learning by our mistakes, so don't feel bad about doing something that went wrong. Instead, learn from it. I did!

After I reunited with my father, I only knew him for about two and a half years, because he fell at his job site and passed away. He was only forty-six years old. The night I found out, I was living in Fountain Valley, California, about an hour south of Los Angeles. I was nineteen years old, and my son was one. It was about 8:00 p.m. I had gone out for a minute, and when I came back, my husband at the time told me, "You need to call your mom. It's about your dad."

I didn't know what to think. At that time in my life, I was in a bad marriage. We were fighting all the time. I was in a very unhealthy marriage. I think I stayed in the marriage because I had my son at such a young age. I didn't even really believe him until I called my mom and she said, "I am on my way down. Your dad is in the hospital." My mom lived an hour away.

I kept saying, "Is he okay? Is he okay?" and she said, "No, it's bad." The day this happened, my dad and I were going to go out to dinner the next day.

When my mom came and got me, we went to the hospital. It was late at night. My dad had just gotten out of surgery. He had to have the left side of his skull removed. When he fell, the impact from the fall had crushed his skull into his brain. The left side of the brain is the part where your motor skills come, your thinking, your balance, your learning to read and write, etc. So my father had no left side of his brain left. He was brain dead at that time.

The hospital was in Los Angeles. I walked in there and saw my dad with a bandage around his whole head, with tubes coming out to drain the excess water from his brain. My dad's head was bigger then a football! Then they moved him to a different hospital where he could get better care. But it didn't help. It made him worse. And he started to get real sick. He was on dialysis. Dialysis is needed when your blood can't filter right through your body; a machine has to do it for you. It pumps the blood out; then it puts it back in. That didn't help either, so they took him to a brain specialist. And that didn't help. So they moved him again to Long Beach Memorial Hospital. Where his condition just got worse.

I said to myself, *It's time to pull the plug, because that's no quality of life.* When we did that, he had been in the hospital for about a month. Then they moved him to a convalescent home where he passed away.

Chapter 3

Where Is My Son?

During the time that I was going in and out of the hospital with my dad, my husband took my son out of state. My son wasn't even a year and a half yet, and I didn't know where he was or if he were dead or alive! So I went to talk to the district attorney about how to get my son back.

The DA told me. "It's going to take a little while to find out where he is." I had given the info about my ex to them: his name, his DOB, his, SSN, his mom's name, etc. I am talking about everything I knew about where he had been and where he might be. It took them about nine months to track him down and then another six months for them to physically go get him.,

Come to find out he was in Maryland, all the way across the country. When they called me to say they had found him, I was dating the man who would become my daughter's dad. He was living in Long Beach, and I was living in Riverside with my mom and step dad. We set up a time to go get my son at the airport. I went, my boyfriend went, and my mom and step dad went. I remember when they handed my son to me; he didn't know who I was! Nor where he was.

He was about two and a half years old. For all of us, it was dramatic! My son had to get used to me again, but that didn't take long. I would have to say it took about one week—max. Ever since then, he has been with my ex or me. So pretty much my ex is his dad. Eventually, he adopted my son. After that, we got married and had our daughter.

Sadly, that did not work out either. By the time I was twenty-three or four, I was twice married and twice divorced, with two kids. At that time, I gave my kids to their dad, because I had gotten into some bad stuff!

HI, MY NAME IS KAMMY, AND I AM A GRATFULLY RECOVERING ADDICT!

Chapter 4

How I Got Started And What I Went Through

I got started using drugs with my first ex-husband, my son's real dad. This was before our child was born. We used to go over to his friends' house, and I could never understand why all his friends and he went into this other room for a few minutes. Until one day I asked him, "Why do you go in that room all the time with them?" and he said, "I do drugs."

I said, "What kind of drugs?" I already knew what pot was, and I knew it was not that. He told me it was meth, so I started to ask questions about what it was like. "What is it like to do it? How's it make you feel?" Stuff like that. So I tried it—he put a little in my drink. I remember it made me stay up for hours. I really felt empowered. At that very moment, I was hooked and didn't even know it. That led into doing lines (snorting it); then that led to smoking it (free-basing). It got really bad from there on out.

Then, when I had my son, I stopped for a while, and then we got divorced. I was by myself for a little while with my son, until I met the man who would become my daughter's dad. Everything was going good for a while—until my addiction caught back up with me. At that time, I didn't think that I had a problem, because it was too new for me to think that I did. But I did!

I blamed a lot of my drug use on my dad dying, when really I was just using that as an excuse to use—I was already hooked. True, I didn't want to deal with my dad dying, and I hid from that for a long time. But I've since learned that it's better in the long run to face whatever it is that you are up against than it is to run and hide.

I used to tell people that I'd go to the store for them. "Just let me use your car." And then I wouldn't come back. My mom used to send me money all the time when I was on the street. Most of it went to my addiction. I used to tell her that I had to pay rent, when really I was living behind a trashcan or at someone's house. It was hard. I never knew where I was going to end up. At that time, my addiction was so bad that I didn't care about what, when, or where—all I cared about was my next *sac*. And who I was going to get it from.

I did a lot of my using with people that I knew. I'll tell you it only takes one person to know fifty people: you know one, you know them all. A lot of my using was done in downtown Long Beach and Riverside. I was at some house one day in Long Beach—I had gone there to go pick up some meth—and a person there owed someone money. One minute I was talking, and the next minute I was on the floor hoping that I wouldn't get shot and die. Six shots came through the window; one shot missed my head by two inches. I felt the air from the bullet whizzing by. And that's all I remember.

I woke up on their kitchen floor, crying. The people in the house said that I had fainted. Then I left. That was the worst thing that I ever went through. But did that stop me? No.

The worst thing that I ever *did* was when my mom went to Hawaii on a trip for two weeks. She had left me with her car, two thousand dollars cash, and said, "Watch the house. I'll see you when I get back. I love you." My mom's husband had just passed away from cancer, and I was living with her in Riverside. She thought I was clean, when really I wasn't. So when she left, in my head I was thinking, Party Time!

My mom was thinking, "She'll be okay; she won't use!"

Then I took her for all she had. One of the people with me was a gang member—I didn't know that at the time—and they took my mom's car, though I didn't know it until I woke up. Then it was too late. So while my mom was thinking everything was okay—the house, the car, and I, she had no clue. When she came home, she had no car, and I was gone too. She tried to get in touch with me but couldn't find me. I didn't talk to my mom for about a year and a half after that. I was too embarrassed and ashamed. Shame had poisoned my inner being.

Finally, when I did talk to her again, we made our peace, and thank God, we did. I put my mom through a lot when I was in my addiction! The longer we allow pain, anger, or disappointment to grow and fester, the more powerful they become. And the more powerful they become, the more they infect our entire beings: our personalities, our attitudes and behaviors, our perspectives, and our relationships. So please let go and let God take care of it.

Pray:

> *God, I pray that I will act wisely in all my ways, and that I will honor you with all my behavior. I thank you for being with me always, causing me to succeed in whatever I am doing, taking me out of the dark, and bringing me into the light.*
> *Amen.*

Related verse—1 Samuel 18:14

Chapter 5

How I Stopped

I finally admitted to myself that I was—and am—powerless over my addiction. Before that, I was thinking that if I went to a couple of meetings, I'd be cured! But no, that's not how it works. I had to go and go and go to meetings and find a sponsor and really be done in my heart. Once I knew deep down inside that I was done, I knew it was God telling me that.

The hardest thing for me was letting go of the people that I had used with. In my mind, they were friends; little did I know that they weren't. They will never be. This time, I had to keep an open mind; otherwise, I would be setting myself up for failure. We have to believe that we can quit and really know that God is on our side every step of the way. Because God goes through whatever we go through first—to see if we can handle it. God does not put anything in front of us that we can't handle.

I used to think that it was impossible for me to quit, but that was the devil saying that to me, and it was me saying, "I can't!" Never say you can't, because you can! I know you can, because I did. So let me encourage you to be aware of your weaknesses and pray regularly for God to strengthen you in the weak spots in your life. This is so moving to me, because I know that you can do it too.

Pray:

> *God, I pray that you will show me your loving kindness and your faithfulness, and that you will strengthen my hands and cause me to be valiant in everything I do in life and everywhere I go.*
> *Amen.*

Related verse—2 Samuel 2:6,7

Chapter 6

Our Addictions Come Back

I was living in Bellflower, California, with my son, my daughter, and her dad. At that time, my son was four and my daughter was about one. Everything was fine until I started working.

I got a job at a nightclub. That's when my life went upside down again. I was a dancer working nights, so I had to stay up somehow. I was really not there for my kids at night or in the day. But I had to take the job, because my husband would never give me money to feed my kids. He would go on these fishing trips for eighteen days at a time.

Don't get me wrong, we always had food in the house, but I never felt like it was enough. At one point, I had to sell my car to feed my kids. I wanted to take my kids to go do little things—like go to the store or go to McDonald's. At that time, we lived by a shopping center, so sometimes I would take my kids there when I had extra money.

The funniest time was when my son wanted to go camping with his best friend Joey. I said, "Okay, we'll go camping!" My son was four at that time, but he still remembers it to this day. Because I didn't have a lot of money at that time, I put a tent up in the backyard. It was a four-man tent, and I said to my son, "Go get the sleeping bags, pillows, and put warm clothes on." So he did. "And go get food!"

He asked, "What about a fire, Mom?"

So we dug a hole in the ground about a half-foot deep and built a fire pit. We got wood, and we went camping. It was so much fun!

I was in and out of my kids' lives for a long time. I was there, but I wasn't. My pattern of drug use was still on-and-off. I used to leave my kids with their dad, and sometimes with my mom, and be gone for days at a time. It started as a couple of hours; hours led to days; days led to weeks, months, and eventually to years. The longest time I was ever gone away from them was two years. At that time, my mom had them. I had to let them go, because I knew that was the right thing to do for them, even though it was hard to do. I didn't want my kids around drugs or around me when I was in my addiction, so I knew that they would be better off with either of them than with me. Deep down inside, I knew I was not ready.

When Satan comes to tempt us to use, he is persistent. He keeps up his attack, hoping to wear us down. And then we do it, the drugs, and then we feel guilty. And that can keep you out there even longer. So pray for help with that temptation to pass, and it will.

Pray:

> *Thank you, God, for delivering me from all who rise up against me and making me strong when I am weak.*
> *Amen.*
>
> Related verse—2 Samuel 18:31

Chapter 7

What We Do To Ourselves And Our Loved Ones

Sometimes, we don't realize what we do because we are so wrapped up in bullshit. We don't take the time to stop and think about what we are doing. We hurt ourselves first, then our loved ones. I was so bankrupted from my experiences that I was unconscious of who I really was and what I was capable of. I put myself through a lot, but I put my loved ones though so much more. Addicts' loved ones sometimes wonder if we are dead or alive! They sometimes say, "Okay, I am not doing this no more!" and they give up on us until we change.

How do you change? Start with recognizing that you have a problem. If it's hard to say no or if you find yourself doing more of whatever it is that you're doing, then you might have a problem. It can be so easy to get caught up in the addiction that we don't see that we have a problem. It all seems so glorious and fun—it's not! It never was.

It's not fun getting stopped by the cops or getting beat up because you made a wrong move. Or getting so high that you see things and talk to things that aren't there. Or doing bad things to other people that you wouldn't do if you weren't high. Or being with someone so you can get your drug of choice when you wish you weren't with them at all. Or getting sick all the time or stealing . . . The list goes on and on until you want to do something about it!

The fun part is . . . there is no fun part about it at all! We just think there is, because we are too high to think any different.

Addicts are filled with self-hatred and self-rejection, as well. So we need to start by forgiving ourselves. You need to learn to really love yourself. It's okay; I know that you can.

Pray:

> *God, I pray that you give me an understanding mind and a heart that hears your voice, so that I can discern between good and evil, and so I never hurt myself or others again.*
>
> *Amen.*

Related verse—2 Kings 3:9

Chapter 8

What My Mom Went Through

My mom got the worst of it. I would have to say more so than my kids. Don't get me wrong, my kids went through it too, and my son remembers more than my daughter does, or anyone else. But my mom saw me go through what I had to go through to get to where I am today and be the woman that I am now. She talked to me over the phone from time to time, until she did me a favor and cut me off.

Cutting me off was the best thing that she ever could have done for me. It made me wake up. She became my worst enemy. Before that, I would call her on the phone and say, "Mom, I have no money to eat," and then she would send me money. Because she believed me, this went on for years, and then I would turn around and spend it on drugs. I ate from time to time, but most of the time I would be too high to eat. My mom always told me back then, "It's never too late to change." That's why half of the title of this book is called It's Never too Late to Change. Because it is not, no matter how old you are!

I have asked my mom what it was like for her. She told me that she doesn't know how I lived. She told me she went to the worst places that she had ever been to in her life trying to get me out of there. When I was in Long Beach, she would see me in the streets with sores on my face. At that time, I was only ninety pounds. I would never go with her until I had made my mind up that I was done! Even then I was not done! My mom has been to drug houses trying to get me out. Did I go with her? No. She has seen me in jail and in downtown Long Beach where lots of people were sleeping on the sidewalks.

My mom said she did a lot of praying to the good lord to help me. And it worked! Thank God it did. I write this book now and look back, saying to myself, That's not the life I want to live ever again. It scares me that I put her life in danger, as well as my own. I could never imagine putting my mom's life in danger today! I did back then because I didn't care about my own life.

So really, think about what you're doing to the people around you before you do anything. It took me a long time to really understand what I was doing to myself and to my loved ones.

Without the right attitude, we can start in the right place and end up in the pit. This happens to a lot of people. To me, this means some people have great opportunities given to them—like second chances with loved ones, education, or work—and yet they do nothing with their lives; they keep going to the pit. Don't let that be you. Don't be vague; be confident! Confident about who you are. And where you want to go in life. I know you can!

Pray:

> *God, I know that you are faithful and that if I ask and keep on asking, I will receive what I need from you. If I seek and keep on seeking, I will find; if I knock and keep on knocking, the door will be opened.*
> *Amen.*

Related verse—Luke 11:10

Chapter 9

What I Go Through Now

It seems to me that I always wanted to rush things in relationships. I think it's from trying to control the people that I was with. When all in all, they weren't the ones for me! When we do drugs, we feel like we have control of ourselves and everything that's around us, when really we are out of control. We have no control over anything—that includes people, places, and things. I have learned that if I am just a little patient things will fall into place right where they need to be. And I will find the one for me. It took me years to grasp this. Once I did, it was life changing!

Now I have the most wonderful person—for now and always. My husband today is someone who understands me and has been down the same road that I have been down. When you have someone who understands you and you understand them, you share a common ground. It makes it easier to talk openly with that person about what you are feeling at any given time, about whatever you're going through. So don't be so eager to be with someone, anyone—give yourself time to really think *IS THIS THE RIGHT ONE FOR ME OR AM I DOING THIS JUST FOR THE TIME BEING?*

God blesses all of us, even though we limp along. We are not perfect, yet he always will work wonders through us in spite of our weaknesses. As you face challenges in your life, beware of thoughts that say, I can't do this; it's just too hard. Don't let your mind give up! That's why it is so important not to lose heart and not to grow weary or faint. You can do this also. You can be sure that wherever God leads you, he is always there, and he is able to keep you. He will never allow more to come on you than you can handle. Amen!

Pray:

God, I thank you for blessing me, watching me, guarding me, and keeping me. Let your face continue to shine upon me and enlighten me. Thank you for being gracious to me and giving me favor. Thank you that your approval is upon that which I do and that which I am. You give me peace.
Amen

Related verse—Numbers 6:24-26

Chapter 10

Feelings And Emotions

Feelings can be deadly if you don't know how to deal with them. Bad ones especially, because those are the ones that can do you and the people around you the most harm. What I mean by this is if you have bad feelings and you don't let them go or talk to someone about them, you will just say I don't care. And I can do what I want when I want without thinking twice about what you're going to do. Or to whom you do it.

Have you ever wondered why we have emotions? Let me tell you why. Because that's how God made us. He wants us to have good feelings all the time—like love for each other, joy, happiness, faith that we can make it, wisdom, courage to carry out everyday strength so we can make it thorough in trying times, peace in our hearts, grace. He does not want us to have bad ones. Satan wants us to have bad ones, like guilt, resentment, shame, no hope, no faith, no love, and so forth.

So let me encourage you to let go of bad feelings. Here's a great exercise: write that person a letter that you are mad at; let them know how you feel about everything you want them to know about—good, bad, it doesn't matter—but don't give it to them. This is for you. Then write another letter that's from them to you about what you would like them to say in response to the first letter you wrote to them.

The first letter that you write will help you let go of feelings about what they did or said or how they were to you, or what you don't like about what they did. The second letter will help you not have the bad feeling about this person because they will say they are sorry about doing whatever they did or saying whatever they said to hurt you to begin with.

Why does this work? Because they really didn't mean to do that bad thing to you in the first place. By doing this, it helps you to release that self-destructive anger that you may have about someone or something or anything else that you are feeling at the time. It helps you to not build up resentment and guilt inside yourself that only hurts you. And it keeps you from doing something that you would regret in the long run. These built-up feelings of anger, resentment, and guilt are among the many things that make us go back out.

There is a time to repress anger, and there is a time to express anger—and wisdom knows the difference. If you are high, you don't have that wisdom. And it takes awhile to develop it. A meek person, in Christian terms, is not someone who never shows anger, but someone who never allows his anger to get out of control. I encourage you to develop true meekness in your life. The word meek means gentle, kind, and humble. By doing so, you should and will inherit the earth.

Pray:

> *Thank you, Jesus, for being faithful and true, for loving me, and for once-and-for-all freeing me from my sins by your own blood. Thank you for helping me to let go of my past and my bad feelings.*
> *Amen.*

Related verse—Revelation 1:5

Chapter 11

Making Mistakes

Mistakes are something that we all make. That's how we learn. Some are bigger than others. The thing is that if you keep making them over and over and never learn, you need to look at that mistake and say to yourself, "Am I going to do that again? Because if I do this, it's not going to make it better. It's going to make it worse! Am I doing the same thing over again that I have done before?" If you keep doing the same thing over and over again, expecting a different result, that's called insanity!

The biggest mistake that I made in the past was blaming my dad for dying, because I had to justify my addiction, find some way to use, but little did I know that was what was harming me and keeping me in the pit. So let me please encourage you to not blame others, because when you do, you are only hurting yourself.

It is really easy to point the finger at someone else, but it is not so easy to say, "This is my fault, and I am wrong." But when you admit that you're wrong, you grow as a person, your inner being becomes healed. Once we learn form our mistakes, it's so nice, because we can say, "Thank you, God, I don't have to go through that again." It took me years to learn this one too. So please don't let your past circumstance become your present reality or who you really are. Let go and let God.

God is always looking for people to promote. That means allowing God to change you. For that, you have to be willing. To be willing, ask him, "Will you change me?" and tell him, "I am ready." The process may hurt at times, but it will help you in the long run. It's okay to make mistakes—just try not to make the same ones over and over again.

Pray:

> *God, thank you for turning curses into blessings in my life because you love me. Thank you for helping me make the right choices and giving me the wisdom to know the difference.*
>
> *Amen.*

Related verse—Deuteronomy 23:5

Chapter 12

Healthy Relationships

Having any relationship can be hard, and it's a lot of work getting to know someone to see if he or she is the right one for you! Sometimes we think that we know someone when we really don't; then you come to find out that he's not the one for you. Then you have to do it all over again; you have to date again to find the right one! So what I think is that you have to get to know yourself first.

Know who you really are deep down inside: what you like and what you don't like, what you will put up with and what you won't. Love yourself first! Really do this for one year before getting involved with anyone. I am not saying you can't have friends; just don't get into a serous relationship. Because without knowing and loving yourself first, you are more apt to find a non-healthy person—because you're not healthy yourself. Know what type of person you really want to be with; then you will be more able to choose a good and healthy relationship, one that you can be with the rest of your life. It took me years to do this.

Ask for wisdom in your relationships, ask God to help you choose the right person for you. I cannot overemphasize the importance of using wisdom as we deal with other people, places, and things. When we ask God for that wisdom, he'll give it to you always!

Pray:

> *Thank you, God, for graciously considering my prayers and supplications and for hearing the requests that I make to help me pick the right one for me.*
> *Amen.*

Related verse—1 Kings 8:28

Chapter 13

Where I Am Today

You know, I am so grateful I am clean today. It took me a lot of years to get here. It took a lot of work to find myself and the person I wanted to be with for the rest of my life, to get to where I want to be, and to regain the things that I had lost for many years. Today I have everything back that was lost! I *did* it! Getting clean was the best thing I ever did for myself . . . and also for my loved ones.

I think that once I finally came to the decision of getting clean, that was it. I was done; no going back. I came to that decision fully only when someone took something from me—my old laptop. That computer had pictures of my family, my dad, and my kids on it that I couldn't replace—you can't go back in time and take pictures like the ones I had on there. It was like my whole life flashed before me, and at that very moment, everything was gone. My life, my kids, my home, my family . . . I was pissed off!

But you know what? I am glad that happened to me. I am so grateful because I don't think that I would have ever stopped using. That was my wake-up call. Thank you, Jesus for that! Today I can't even imagine going back to where I was. I say to myself, *How did I really get though what I experienced?!* I know that it was God that saw me through; without him by my side, I could never have made it. He is the one that helped me write this book to help others, and I know that he will see you through too! All you have to do is give yourself a chance. I hope this book helps you look at what drugs will do to you and your loved ones if you keep using.

Pray:

> *Thank you, God, for being on my side today. Thank you for giving me courage and strength. Thank you for the revelation of your presence in my life. Thank you for leading me to where I am at today.*
> *Amen*

Related verse—1 Kings 8:43

Chapter 14

Doing Something You've Never Done Before

You know getting clean is one of the hardest things you'll ever do. You have to really want it. You have to really be *done* in your heart. Sometimes people have a wake-up call like I had; sometimes, it's worse and something bad happens to you. Some people don't make it at all, and they die. I know if I could do it, so can you. Here is how:

When your body first gets clean or sober, you go though what is called the DTs (*delirium tremens*). That means your body is telling you *I want more!*—of whatever it was that you were using. You feel like you don't want to do anything. You want to sleep. And you want to eat and then go back to bed. The reason for this is because we have a chemical (a neurotransmitter) called *dopamine* in our brains. That's what wakes us up everyday and what makes us feel good. When we use drugs or alcohol, the correct levels of dopamine drop, so instead of feeling good and energetic, you feel tired and want to sleep all the time. You get depressed.

Well, the good news is that it rights itself a little every day that you stay clean and sober. If you get clean for a week, but then you go back out, it becomes harder to go back to getting clean. Because your body is telling you it needs more than you gave it the last time you used. That's why, once you make that decision to get clean or sober, you need to stay with it. Don't give up! In the long run, you will feel so much better about yourself, and your loved ones will too! Not only that, but *you'll get your looks back* . . . and, funny thing, so will your loved ones!

You know that new things always seem frightening, but soon they become old things, and God will put another "new thing" on the horizon of our lives. We need to grow accustomed to stepping out and into new things. The more we do, the more we realize that it's okay to change.

In order to take hold of new things, we must let go of the old things like people, places, and things that don't work for us, in order to get acquainted with the new. Say to yourself, "Thank you, God, that you love me, that you are holding me in your hands, that I can follow you and receive direction for my life from you.

Pray:

> *Thank you, God, that you have girded me with strength for every battle that I face. Thank you for a new day, every day.*
> *Amen.*

Related verse—2 Samuel 22:40

Chapter 15

No Matter Where You Go . . .

No matter where you go, it's always there if you really want it. So say like you have one month clean and sober and you get the feeling that you want to say *F–it*, 'cause something ain't going the way you want it to go. Or say you moved away to get away from it, because deep down inside you wanted to stay clean, and then you walk down the street and *bam!* It's there. Are you going to do it? Or are you going to say to yourself, "You know, it took me so long to get this one mouth clean and sober, and I feel so good and look like a million bucks, I don't need this; I am better than this," and then you walk away?

To me, getting this was hard, because when I moved from place to place, or from town to town, it was always there. I tried to get away from it, because I really wanted to stay clean, so I finely realized that no matter where I went or what state I was in, it was always going to be there if I wanted it! So this is how it works: CHASE YOUR RECOVERY LIKE YOU WOULD CHASE YOUR DRUGS. *This means go seek out meetings!* Get on the phone and call the NA[1] hotline to find a meeting near you, get a sponsor, and do whatever it takes for your recovery! In the long run, it's worth it.

Whatever your situation is, know that God promises to go with you. Trust God that he will give you favor and the strength to give you the right words to speak in every situation in a loving way when the time comes.

---

[1]   Narcotics Anonymous (To find your local hotline number, go to http://www. na.3org/.)

Pray:

God, I declare that in you, I am not lacking in any spiritual endowment or Christian grace. Thank you for establishing me to that end and giving me strength to say no.

Amen.

1 Corinthians 1:7,9

Chapter 16

My Strength

My strength is my loving god, my meetings, and my NA friends. Writing this book also gives me strength to help others, because it helps me look back and remind myself of who I was, where I came from, and who I really am deep down. You always want to remember who you are and where you came from, that you are an addict who climbed back from it, but still an addict. Because you are never really recovered, you are never *cured*; you will always be an addict, but you can be a RECOVERING one if you make that change!

Without God on my side, I could not have done this. I could not have done this alone. I know that I can turn to God when I am in a bad mess or if something is wrong or if I need anything and say, "God, I come to you to help me with what I am going through. Walk before me and help see me through. Amen."

The bible tells us that God is a spiritual being and those who worship him must worship him in spirit *and* truth. And in order to hear his voice, we must believe in him (John 4:24). When we are "born again," we are made alive in our spirits to be sensitive to the voice of God. Then we can hear him whisper, even though we cannot tell where this still, small voice comes from. But I will tell you: it comes from deep down within our hearts. Just believe that he is there for you too and he will hear you.

Pray:

> *Thank you, God. I have peace because you are helping*
> *me. And you're with me no matter where I go.*
> *Amen.*

1 Chronicles 12:18

Chapter 17

My Hope

I hope this book has given you the encouragement to be whatever it is that you want to be! And to do all the things that you want to do in life. And to make that change for yourself first. There are going to be a lot of things that you're going to have to sacrifice and do that you've never done before. There are going to be ups and downs and feelings that you never felt before. I hope that I never have to go through what I went through again Because it was not a good thing. I know if I stick around the rooms of recovery, pray to God everyday to give me the wisdom and strength to hang out with people that are clean today and to change people, places, and things that aren't good for me, that I will be fine. And so will you!

Make that change for yourself, because I know you can!

Pray:

> God, thank you, for giving me the experience, strength, and hope that I can do this and that I am not alone. Thank you for seeing me through.
> In Jesus's name, amen.

What To Do When You Have A Child With An Addiction Problem

I know that it is hard to deal with when you have a child or a loved one that is going through an addiction problem. Because you want to help them and be there for them as much as you can, it's important you don't turn into their enabler. The thing is that you can be there, but it means you have to stand your ground and be strong for yourself first, You might have to say no to whatever it is that they want—because they will try to manipulate you to get it and then turn around and do it again. If they are addicts, they know that if the first time worked, the second time will too, and that pattern will just get worse.

You have a choice—either you get to the point where you say okay and give in just to get them do what you want them to do, or you say, "I am done, and I want you out of my life until you get help." This choice is the only one that will help you and your loved ones going through their addiction. You can't keep going through this with them; it's bad for your health—your body, your state of mind, and your inner being. And you help them stop when you stop helping them. It helps them if they are the type who has to hit rock bottom first. I am talking about the addict who has to lose *everything* before they are done. I know this, because I went through it, and this is what my mom had to do with me.

Everybody's *bottom* is different. It could be food, money, loved ones, the roof over their heads, their kids, their jobs, and on and on. The saddest thing is that some people don't ever get this chance to live to tell about how they stopped. As a parent, I hope that I have given you some encouragement to be strong for you and your loved ones.

Pray:

Thank you, God, for all you do for me and my loved ones. Thank you for giving me the courage to stand strong in my trying times. Thank you for the wisdom to know what to say and how to go about drawing the line when the time comes.

In the name of Jesus, amen.

Chapter 19

The Letter To My Dad In Heaven

Dear Dad,

I miss you so much! I know that we never got a chance to really get to know each other. I know that I was always your daughter, and I will always be, now and forever. When you left me, it was hard for me to deal with, because I was so young. I needed my dad. I went to live on your boat thinking that I would be close to you and you would come back, but you didn't. I am sorry that I sold the boat, but I had to.

I know that Mom did what she had to do to take care of me. So *please* don't be mad at her—she is the best mom a daughter could ever have. I am so blessed to have her.

Mom has been though a lot with me. I had a problem with drugs for a long time, but I am better now. It took me a lot of years to get to where I'm at today, Dad. You would be so proud of me.

Hey, your grandson, Timmy, is so big! The last time you saw him he was a baby. Now he is almost eighteen years old! He is so handsome, Dad. He loves fishing and boats just like you did—he wants to be a captain of one someday. I know he will be just like you were.

Timmy's dad and me are no longer together. I know that you would be happy about this, 'cause I knew that you never liked him—you just never told me, but I always knew deep down inside. So I got a divorce.

I got married again and had a little girl. Her name is Leah. She is so beautiful! I named her after Grandma Dora's mom. She loves horses. Me and *her* dad didn't work out either, so we went are separate ways. But the cool thing, Dad, is that we are friends—for the kids. I am sorry that you and mom weren't. But if you think about it, you were there for a little while, until you left this world and went to another. I guess you had to go take care of other stuff up there. I know that we will see each other some day!

Oh, by the way, Mom is doing well. She has her own business now—she does facials. She is really good at it too. She had to go to school for that. She had a hard time with passing the test at first, but she did not give up, and she has her license now. She is remarried to a great guy who has his own company. He has three sons, so I have three stepbrothers, but you know what, dad, I think of them like they were my real brothers! Mom has been with him for a long time now.

Oh, by the way, Dad, tell Grandma and everybody that's up they're with you I said hi and I miss them too!!

Now back to me. I just want to tell you that I got married again. Ya, I know, it's my third time, but you know what they say: "Third time's a charm!" By the way, the first times don't count in my book! Ha-ha. The man I married now, he is the best thing that's ever happened to me, Dad. He has been down the same road I have; he treats me really good. We have so much fun together—he gives me lots of love, and he will take good care of me. Plus, he is my soul mate. I know that if you were to meet him you would fell the same way about him as I do!

I love you very much. It was nice to write you this letter to let you know how everything is going in my life today . . . Talk to you later.

Love you always,
Your daughter,
Kammy D. Howard

Chapter 20

The Letter From My Dad To Me

Dear Kammy

This is your dad. I am sorry that I had an accident at work. I know that it must have been hard for you and your mom, especially because of the things that you were going though at the time it happened. I am sorry that I was not there for you when you needed me the most.

My work on earth was done, and I had to go up there and hang some drywall—ha—for my house in heaven and the good lord's too! I am glad to hear that you're doing well and my grandkids are too and so is your mom. You know that I was upset for a long time about what your mom did to me when she garnisheed my wages, but I am over it. I love you and your mom, and I wish nothing but good for you guys!

I am so glad that you guys have the best and that you overcame your addiction to drugs, Kammy, 'cause if I'd been there, I would have put my foot up your butt!

Well, tell your mom that everybody says hi up here. Talk to you later.

Love,
Your dad
Steven B. Howard

Chapter 21

The Letter Back To My Dad

Dear Dad

Thank you for writing me that letter, Dad. It helps—except you being gone, 'cause for a long time there, I had a hard time dealing with it! That's one of the reasons that I blamed my using on—you being gone—when really, I had the problem.

I am glad that you're in a better place now, up there with your mom, and that there are some other people that you know too. When I came to the hospital, you weren't looking so good, so I am glad that you don't have to go though that pain anymore. Mom and me had to make the decision to pull the plug, because we knew that you would not want to live like that one more day! So we set you free. I hope that you're doing good. Say hi to Grandma for me, and . . . thank you for being one of my angels. I love you, Dad.

Well, it was nice writing back to you. Thank you once again for helping me understand why!

Love you always,
Your daughter,
Kammy D Bowman